THERE WILL ALWAYS BE NIGHTS LIKE THIS

Published by Cipher Press
www.cipherpress.co.uk
@cipherpress

ISBN: 978-1-9163553-3-0

Featuring: Isabel Waidner, Mads Hartley, Peter Scalpello,
Elizabeth Lovatt, Saurabh Sharma, Sam J Grudgings, Cleo
Henry, Erica Gillingham, Gabrielle Johnson, Helen Savage,
Adam Zmith, Georgie Henley, Annie Dobson

Design by Wolf @ keepingthewolvesatbay.co.uk

Typeset by Laura Jones

Edited by Ellis K. & Jenn Thompson

Printed and bound in the UK by Ex Why Zed

**Any profits made from the sale of this book
will be donated to The Outside Project**

Contents

Isabel Waidner

How to Run a Queer Reading Series at a LDN Arts Institution

'*Queers Read This* is a literature event that isn't boring.'

Queers Read This is an ongoing reading series started independently by artist Richard Porter and myself at the Horse Hospital in London in 2017, and co-run with the Institute of Contemporary Arts (ICA) since. Quarterly events feature readings of texts which work across intersectional systems of oppression, and challenge formal distinctions between prose and poetry or critical and creative writing. Themes range from pansies and twink mysticism (Caspar Heinemann), sissy bois (Natasha Lall), art in black homes (Abondance Matanda), and protection spells against magpies (Timothy Thornton), to the end of the world (Alison Rumfitt). Alongside like-minded reading series organised by The 87 Press, the *No Matter* poetry series in Manchester, and *Horseplay* in Brighton for example, *Queers Read This* has been instrumental in re-defining inter-disciplinary writing as a medium which is bringing together new communities of LGBTQI+, Black, BAME and working-class writers, poets, artists, performers and readers in the UK. The title of the series is gratefully borrowed from an anony-mously published leaflet distributed at a 1990 Pride march in New York.

This fan fiction essay introduces the best of *Queers Read This*, and recruits it into a blockbuster narrative. Written prior to the Covid-19 pandemic, it strangely anticipates the loss or suspension of institutional access and queer sociality. Though unprecedented in terms of its universality, the current suspension feels like an extension of the precarity and ephemerality of queer working-class infrastructures at the best of times.

The multidimensional theatre space is huge, black walls. When I say multidimensional I mean several past and future *Queers Read This* and related events are collapsed into one, and unreeled simultaneously—busy night. The foot high, square stage in the middle of the theatre is surrounded by seats on all sides like a boxing ring. Early audience members and readers are wandering around, talking. Event curators are chatting to techies. A test puff of dry ice goes up in the air. Some people are coughing, or, if ever they personally or on TV experienced a house fire, potentially triggered—international guest star Dodie Bellamy is reminded of the California wildfires, Autumn '18. A smoke machine isn't innocent, not in relation to PTSD! I understand now that there are small, controlled fires in each corner of the theatre.

The place is filling up. Happy hardcore plays quietly in the background. Mojisola Adebayo, Helen Cammock and Abondance Matanda sit down in the back row, furthest away from the entrance. Clay AD, Huw Lemmey, R. Zamora Linmark, D. Mortimer and Kashif Sharma-Patel sit in the first row, nearest the entrance. I get up on stage. Test one, two. Joanna Walsh there, Timothy Thornton. Shola von Reinhold! But what's this. There, in the back. I see an arm in a neoprene wetsuit, a neon-green gardening glove. Another arm, three, four in total. Gone. Let's hope I'm imagining things, it's my job after all. Roz! I hop off the stage to say hi to Roz Kaveney. At the edge of my vision, I see a figure in neoprene creep up behind people in the back row, left. IT'S THE EXTRA-TERRESTRIAL VORTEX QUEEN FROM LINDA STUPART AND CARL GENT'S DIY ARTISTS' PLAY *ALL OF US GIRLS HAVE BEEN DEAD FOR SO LONG*, WHICH, OF ALL PLACES, PREMIERED HERE IN THE ICA THEATRE LAST JUNE! Know that this place hasn't always been multidimensional. At one point during Stupart and Gent's play, the Vortex Queen unleashed a significant vortex in the venue's then regular theatre space, multiplying dimensions. I watched it happen, own eyes.

Place is getting packed. Another puff of dry ice, the Vortex Queen lives for dry ice. Dry ice is the reason why she decided to occupy the theatre in the first place. Originally derived from the 1992 *Ecco The Dolphin* SEGA video game, the Vortex Queen abstracts natural resources from the Earth like a venture capitalist, syphoning raw material off our planet via gigantic vortices. With the planet's resources largely depleted, she, in 2020, has evolved to metabolise toxic by-product and waste, including dry ice and preferably urban human bodies.

I signal my co-host, let's open the night. Porter and I get up on stage. Music stops. Spotlights come on. We banter, tell the audience who and what to expect. We laugh, the audience laugh, implicit gay trauma connecting us all. That's why our laughter is so wild and so free, like pink smoke billowing from barely controlled fires.

Verity Spott, the Brighton-based poet, steps onto the stage. We are honoured, et cetera. Like every reader at *Queers Read This*, Spott rotates on stage as she reads, addressing different sections of the audience in turn. I'm concerned that the rotating motion, recurrent at that, should open some kind of metaphysical borehole, and that's on top of the temporal vortex we're already living the consequences of. Reading her poem in which madness, more specifically Suggs from Madness, creeps up on her grandmother, Spott brings the house down. Reading another poem which connects the BBC to the Gender Recognition Act or its potential reform (from *Prayers, Bravery, Manifestos*, 2019), Spott walks over the rubble of the house she already brought down, crushing it. Standing ovation for Verity Spott! Amid the cheers, nobody seems to see what I see. The Vortex Queen tackles one of the few working-class audience members in the room and tears out their working-class heart.

Next up, Nisha Ramayya. Poet reads *Future Flowers*, from her collection *States of the Body Produced by Love* (2019). The poem starts with hundreds of thousands of albatrosses courting and ends up with the real fucking police sitting across the street from a real fucking temple in Hyderabad. En route, it discusses the race to "one-pointed consciousness", the opening of the hole in one's head into which "sky drips", and other actions conducive to the imagination. *Future Flowers* speaks of the want to be left alone with one's mind-rays, a cosmic puppet, dangling in the grandeur of the inner void. But how to achieve perfect desirelessness when surrounded by kissy noises? "Everyone and everything is kissing," Ramayya reads, "except you! Your mouth is stuffed full of flowers and even these flowers are kissing each other, inside your mouth as if you were simply a space in which desire takes place." Nisha! This is exactly what *Queers Read This* feels like at its best!

I first heard Ramayya read *Future Flowers* the year before at a student-organised reading at a post-'92 university. I, writer, borrowed a perceived image from the poem of two lions vomiting. In my novel *We Are Made Of Diamond Stuff* (2019) the lions' vomit rises into the air where the distinct streams meet and create a giant vomit heart in the sky. The vomit heart turns into a lasso and is being weaponised against the border police. Hearing *Future Flowers* again now, I can say that, on top of the topics already mentioned, it covers coloured powders, corpse-width bodies, and, crucially, lions, but no flying vomit hearts. The lions that do appear in *Future Flowers* don't vomit—they prop open their mouths with enemy heads. This, is speaking to me. I should bite the Vortex Queen's head off, stop her from clawing out proletarian hearts.

She beats me to it. It's the Vortex Queen who ends up biting the head off of a precarious audience member, fourth or fifth row, exit-facing! ENOUGH! I leap onto the stage, interrupting Ramayya's reading. I take the microphone, alarm! Alarm! "The Vortex Queen is killing lovers of literature!" I say. The audience look at me, stunned. "Let's stop her, I beg!" The audience start to boo a little, they prefer their poetry readings unpunctuated. They don't believe, they say, that the, what, Fostex King?, is killing liter-ature? "The VORTEX QUEEN," I correct, "is killing LOVERS of literature." Where, by the way, is she, is she hiding. "What about the corpse-width body," I say, pointing to what's left of it in row five. Are we to call the police?! No. No police. Four audience members get up, pick up the body and bury it under the row of seats. So there, wipe wipe, they wash their hands of it. Can Nisha Ramayya get back on stage and finish her reading now. Ok wow. I let that sink it. It's not that the audience are unscrupulous, reckless and classist, I think. They're just really committed to cutting edge poetry.

Fine. I'm on my own. I'll end the nefarious Vortex Queen solo, send her two-bit, I mean, 16-bit butt back to the 1990s alone. Question is how.

Ramayya cannot be persuaded to continue her reading right now, so Porter and I introduce our next reader, Natasha Lall. In Lall's *The 16mb, Future Sounds & A Mini City* (2018), a trilogy of lo-fi, retro-futurist videos shot in Glasgow, a protagonist (Lall), sometime in the post-apocalyptic future, searches for the meaning and origin of an obscure, obsolete object, a 16mb memory card. On their quest, they come across other forgotten objects, like a golden snow globe containing the titular mini city. Lall discovers that the memory card would have been used to store information. What if crucial insights are contained on there, such as the histories leading up to the apocalypse? The reasons behind the general absence of memory cards and snow globes in future Glasgow? There is no electricity in this dystopia, but Lall works on cracking the 16mb using a circuit diagram, rubber bands, sellotape, mechanical forces and magic.

They got something. On an ancient Atari in a Glaswegian bedroom, a message appears: 'To rid yrself of th EVIL Vo tex Qu.' Blank screen. Sellotape manipulation produces: 'follo these instru©ti◻ns.' Power out. Say what? Can it be that a 16mb memory stick in the retrofuture contains detailed instructions for the removal of the Vortex Queen from a multi-dimensional theatre space? The exact how-to? Yes, it can! Lall gets their head down. Access to the stored data is ever more urgent.

Meanwhile, Huw Lemmey gets up on the ICA stage and reads communist pornography, or, his novel *Red Tory: My Corbyn Chemsex Hell* (2019). In it, protagonist Tom, a moderate member of Oxford University Gay Labour Youth and aspiring career politician enters the LDN chemsex scene, partly to process what he perceives to be the Labour Party's counterproductive turn towards basically communism following Corbyn's election as leader in 2015. In an interview with *i-D*, Lemmey describes the satirical conceit of *Red Tory* as follows: "[W]hat if the tabloid newspapers' [overblown and reductive] descriptions of the political scene in the UK were reality?" Playing on the real-life media's belief that ordering a latte in Costa was the epitome of middle-class culture, cappuccino actually is elitist in *Red Tory*, for example. And the people who joined the Labour Party in 2015 are the bloodthirsty communists the media made them out to be. But at its best, *Red Tory* performs the more nuanced ways in which hard facts and imaginaries fundamentally co-shape contemporary reality. Take the pig sex scene early on in the novel: In a newly-built block of flats in East London, Tom experiences chemically induced hallucinations of being fucked by "daddy pig", whose "body seemed enormous and pink, so very pink." "The piggy rocked back and forth," and then, after what seems like a period of extensive "assfucking", piggy grew "so tall his trotters, raised up above his head, ripped down the halogen chandelier, bringing shards of the ceiling with it."

Oh, CRAAAAASH!!! That's the Vortex Queen tearing down, not a halogen chandelier in an East London fuck flat, but a heavy-weight spotlight in the ICA theatre. Parts of the ceiling come down with it. No audience members were hurt, but one of the small, inadequately controlled fires is now out of control. Pink smoke everywhere. Vision is overall poor, but some audience members are prepared to admit that they ~may~ have seen ~something like~ the Vortex Queen taking down part of the ceiling. Lemmey holds it together, continues reading:

Having passed out after the piggy sex orgy, *Red Tory's* Tom gets up and walks into a local newsagent. He sees the headlines 'Prime Minister Pigfucker', 'CAMERON HUMILATED BY PIG SEX SCANDAL', and 'CAMERON: CONFIRMED PIG FUCKER'. Tom thinks he is still hallucinating, still tripping on Tina or meth— of course #piggate actually happened. I, for one, have resigned myself to the twilight affair that is facto-fiction at this historical juncture in Britain, and also to the fact that there's pigs everywhere.

Intent on infiltrating, colonising and flying like so many proverbial piglets, the Vortex Queen gets up on stage. She starts bounding on the spot, gently at first, then increasingly vigorously, sending shock waves through the theatre like a minor earthquake. But what's this, the extra-terrestrial's neoprene skin begins to blister. She can't take the heat on stage, I think, but that isn't it. Tiny Vortex Princelets are hatching from bursting blisters, dozens of them. They detach from the parental body and take flight! They're nothing like piglets, they are albatrosses crowding the air. Poetry lovers are fighting them off with their phones like lightsabres. Remember when we were all kissy kissy? Not now. Re-enacting the albatross fest in *Future Flowers*, we are "hundreds of thousands of awkward bodies, golden arms, sword-fighting, sunbeams, laser quests." We "hold hands, rub beaks, play footsie, […] wind tails together, […] bumpity bump bump bump." Literature fans and Vortex Princelets "circle each other, full body popping; […] [we] star-gaze." We are one communal body, except we aren't "[t]he absolute soul of the universe," which according to Ramayya is "an assemblage of migratory birds, whose agitation is indeed creation." We are an absurdly poetic battlefield.

Back in the retrofuture, Lall has been working on accessing the memory card's content sans electricity. Latest phrase appearing on the screen is: 'You want t◻ imagine futures?' "It's the opening line of *Future Flowers*," Porter says, ducking. Vortex Princelets are dive bombing from the ceiling, winning their fight against battery-intensive lightsabres run off our phones. "What is," I ask. "You want to imagine futures," Porter repeats. "It's the opening line of Ramayya's *Future Flowers*." Turns out, Nisha Ramayya didn't read the opening line of her poem earlier tonight. Before she was interrupted, she read *Future Flowers* BACKWARDS, honouring the temporal idiosyncrasies distinguishing this particular event. Is the 16mb telling us that the deactivation of the Vortex Queen is connected to the end, I mean, the beginning of *Future Flowers*?! The part we haven't yet heard? "Hey!" I make myself heard over the sword-fighting, the laser questing. (Mythologically speaking, it is very unlucky to kill albatrosses.) *"Future Flowers,"* I say. You what? *"Future Flowers,"* I insist. Finally! The audience are glad I've come 'round to their way of thinking. They've wanted Ramayya's poetry all along.

A million gold flakes are falling from the ceiling as if the theatre were a snow globe and we were a mini city. Incinerated Vortex Princelets? Torched PVC chairs? Acid rain? Chemtrails? We've got to act now—.

Every writer and poet in the room drops their phone-y weapon and gets up on stage. In concert, Mojisola Adebayo, Dodie Bellamy, Helen Cammock, Roz Kaveney, Natasha Lall, Huw Lemmey, R Zamora Linmark, Abondance Matanda, D. Mortimer, Richard Porter, Nisha Ramayya, Shola von Reynolds, Verity Spott, Timothy Thornton, Joanna Walsh, Eley Williams and I resume reading *Future Flowers* where Ramayya left off. I can confirm that no lions vomit in the early parts of the poem either, nor do vomit hearts take to the sky—that's just me, just *We Are Made Of Diamond Stuff.* But at the very end of our collective reading, the actual beginning of *Future Flowers*, two elephants feature, vomiting rainbows. The rainbows meet and, YES, they fuse in the air to form a giant lunette! A lunette (*n.*) is a crescent-shaped object, an area enframed by an arch, and also a peephole. The Vortex Queen turns her head in my direction exactly—.

IS THE PEEPHOLE THE ANTI-VORTEX? IS THE PEEP-HOLE THE GATEWAY THROUGH WHICH TO TRANSPORT THE VORTEX QUEEN BACK TO THE 1990S? I think so! Coinciding with our second or third collective iteration of the word 'lunette', a whirl like a giant pink piglet's tail materialises in the theatre. Within seconds, the anti-vortex, or peephole, or piglet's tail claims the Vortex Queen and everything else alive or dead, except me. I'm left in an empty theatre. No writers, no audience, no pink smoke billowing. No uncontrolled fires, no puffs of dry ice. No happy hardcore playing quietly, no curators, no co-host, no *Queers Read This.* The anti-vortex took everything away, sent it back to various points in the past and the future. I would raid the ICA bookshop on my way out, but even the books are gone.

Acknowledgements

Thanks to Cipher Press for publishing. Thanks to everyone involved in any way in making *Queers Read This* happen, especially Richard Porter, Rosalie Doubal, Sara Sassanelli and our readers. Thanks to our audiences. Scheduled on 2 April 2020, Queers Read This (5) was postponed indefinitely, as was every other queer and literary physical get-together worldwide. List of events referenced in the text:

Queers Read This(1), 24 May 2018 at ICA, London. With Richard Porter, Abondance Matanda, Nisha Ramayya, Timothy Thornton, Isabel Waidner and Joanna Walsh. Music by Charlie Porter.

Queers Read This (2), 16 November 2018 at ICA, London. With Dodie Bellamy, Natasha Lall, Richard Porter, Verity Spott and Isabel Waidner.

Queers Read This (3), 7 March 2019 at ICA, London. With Helen Cammock, Caspar Heinemann, D. Mortimer, Richard Porter and Isabel Waidner.

Queers, Class and the Avant-garde, 23 May 2019 at ICA, London. Presented by writer Isabel Waidner, this evening of readings and discussion interrogated queerness and class in interdisciplinary writing and publishing in the UK, and featured presentations by Mojisola Adebayo, Ray Filar, Roz Kaveney, Huw Lemmey and Kashif Sharma-Patel.

Queers Read This (4), 7 November 2019 at ICA, London. With Clay AD, R. Zamora Linmark, Richard Porter, Alison Rumfitt, Shola von Reinhold and Isabel Waidner.

Queers Read This (5), 2 April 2020 [POSTPONED]. With Sophia Al-Maria, Harry Burgess, Danielle Brathwaite-Shirley, Richard Porter, Tai Shani and Isabel Waidner.

Bibliography

Burke, Harry (2019) 'A Satirical Slice of Pro-communist Erotic Fan Fiction'. In *i-D*, 17 June 2019, https://i-d.vice.com/en_uk/article/8xze5k/red-tory-my-corbyn-chemsex-hell-interview-huw-lemmey

Lall, Natasha (2018) *The 16mb, Future Sounds & A Mini City.* Video.

Lemmey, Huw (2019) *Red Tory: My Corbyn Chemsex Hell.* London: Montez Press.

Ramayya, Nisha (2019) 'Future Flowers.' In *States of the Body Produced by Love.* London: Ignota Books.

Spott, Verity (2019) *Prayers, Bravery, Manifestos.* London: Pilot Press.

Stupart, Linda & Gent, Carl (forthcoming) *All Of Us Girls Have Been Dead For So Long.*

Waidner, Isabel (2019) *We Are Made Of Diamond Stuff.* Manchester: Dostoyevsky Wannabe.

Body Matter

I last had a night out on March 7. Moth Club was filled to capacity — 300 people — and Héloïse Letissier of Christine and the Queens was shouting *'What quarantine?'*. The crowd cheered back at her. She brought out Caroline Polachek, who later turned out to have coronavirus, for a duet, and the pair of them bounced around the stage together, fizzing with tension, getting close enough to kiss more times than I could count.

I got drunk on pricey double gin and tonics and let my friend give me a huge temporary tattoo as we waited for the gig to start. I pulled up the sleeve of my T-shirt and, with one set of fingers on my forearm, she pressed a wad of damp toilet roll to my bicep. The cold water dripping into my watch strap reminded me of the sweat pooling on the small of my back, of how close the air around us was. I had to scrape the tattoo off in the bath a week later, tired of being a walking *La Vita Nuova* advert, but it clung to me like it was my own skin.

After the gig I decided not go to on to a queer night in Hackney Wick. My ex would be there, and I knew we'd both be drunk. I'd agonised over it for weeks, but the fear of seeing her too soon after we'd broken up and risking the friendship we'd established, still tentative, held me back. When I first saw the photos from that night, I was hit with a pang of envy. Later, the group I planned to go with realised that each one of them had ended up ill soon after, lain up in bed with ragged lungs, taste and smell on extended leaves of absence.

Instead of hugging dozens of people and sharing keys with a select few, that night I went home with someone I'd been on a couple of dates with. As I leaned against the wall of the Glory, I reached out to her, gripped the corner of her corduroy jacket. I pulled her towards me unconsciously, for the first time not shy about making clear how much I wanted her as soon as I saw her. We held hands in the cab back to my flat, letting our fists take up the middle seat.

The next morning, under bedding I'd bought to mark moving house, still slightly scratchy, we lay facing one another, eyes shut. She touched my clit, her fingers flicking left and right. Sensing that I wanted more, she reached her other hand between my legs to fuck me. I moved against her, having no sense of how loud I was being or what my face was doing. Afterwards I had the drunken sensation that sometimes accompanies that particular kind of sex — the kind that's almost an out-of-body experience — and told her, uninvited, probably slurring, how good she'd made me feel. When she left I said 'see you soon' and believed that I would.

●

Seven weeks later and part of me believes I'd get that drunken sensation now, not from fucking in the morning sunlight with someone whose body was still new to me, whose body I'd quietly longed for — now I could evaporate, practically, from a kiss. Specifically, the second kiss: the type that comes after the dry, halting meeting of closed lips, the first glimpse of your tongue meeting another's, that soft, warm, wet, nanosecond which, even if the timing or pressure or angle is off, sends a shock to your stomach.

Now I wake up under that same bedding, alone and irritated. The blind that was broken when I moved in is still broken, and waking up early and reaching for a lover feels quite different to waking up early and alone and reaching for the eye-mask I keep on the spare pillow. This bedding I bought, the symbol of new beginnings, is no longer new, and it has made psoriasis like pink waterlilies bloom across my chest. I lie in a bath full of Epsom salt and, afterwards, gloss my body with a steroid serum that sticks to me like dripping. If I forget to wash my hands after-wards my glasses are shot for the day. If I put clothes on too quickly, the residue lines my bra and my shirt.

I've been lucky enough not to get ill and privileged enough to be furloughed on full pay, but now my days sprawl like ivy. I haven't adapted to getting dressed being the final step of my morning routine. Spending this much time naked doesn't come naturally to me, and, as far as I can remember, never has done. I dry my hair in front of the mirror, positioned in such a way that I can't see my chest or my groin. I practise the dumbbell routine I've adopted in the hopes of coming out of lockdown with a stronger, wider, leaner body. Each time, as I lift the weights above my shoulders and my head drops, I'm struck by the actual fact of my body.

When my life was a whirring rotation of work, socialising, and sleep, the disconnect I felt from my physical self could easily be shuffled to the back of my mind. Ignoring my body had been so normal, for so long, that the disconnect felt almost inconsequential. Now, forced to face myself as I am, the truth is stark and unsettling: an unwelcome visitor, usually fleeting, has turned resident. One morning I take action and email a private doctor who can prescribe testosterone.

Dysphoria hits me in strange ways. I had almost convinced myself I didn't experience it, only to realise that, in fact, I have spent my life so far working *around* my body. My appearance has been specially honed so that when I look in the mirror fully clothed, I feel content. Unclothed, all bets are off. Any type of human contact can exacerbate or dissipate my discomfort, but sex is what shunts me to the extremes of both states.

At worst, I am hyperaware of my body, banned from feeling pleasure, no matter how gentle or rough or inventive the partner. I feel each movement so keenly that un-tensing, 'switching off', seems as simple as clicking my fingers and finding my body reconstructed. At best, I am unaware of myself, almost transcendent. Sometimes, very rarely, I feel pleasure not in spite of my body, but because of it. This, the facing of my feminine body head-on and not finding it wanting, finding it the opposite of wanting, stuns me each time.

The doctor offers me an appointment in mid July. I know, logically, that this decision has been less like seven weeks and more like seven years in the making, and has finally fought its way to the surface now that I've been forced to stand still. And yet I worry that the confidence I feel about changing my body — a confidence that has solidified while I have been lacking distractions, yes, but also lacking the touch of others — might crumble the next time I am close to another person.

It is a cliché to describe sex as transformative. In my case, though, sex has the potential to be transformative and, simultaneously, its opposite — it is the one thing that has the power to hold me present in the body I have spent a lifetime trying to avoid.

Seven weeks later, I'd take my teeth bumping into someone else's, twenty times; I'd take an ac-cidental bite on the labia, five times (max); I'd take ten conversations in a dusky beer garden, the breeze finally turning chill on my bare legs as I'm told that we want different things, if it meant I got to go on one good first date this summer. I'd take them all twice over if we met — safely, somehow — during a night out, in a club where the ceiling was low enough, and the people were tightly packed enough, that the walls dripped with sweat and the bass felt like my heartbeat.

When she arrives, early evening, the sun is searing my scalp. She takes a seat across from me and I find myself chipping away at the surface of our picnic bench, risking splinters with each thrust of my thumb. When she passes me a pint her handprint is visible on the glass, cut through the condensation. She talks me through her lockdown, lists the people she knows who were ill, explains how she is adjusting to being back in an office of sixty, and grins at me over the rim of her glass as she sips her beer. We order fries, speckled with rock salt and rosemary, then lick the grease from our lips. I reach for her hand under the table and our fingers meet, passing minuscule crystals of salt back and forth. As we stand to leave I see her press the flesh between her thumb and forefinger to her mouth to clean it and feel dizzy at the peek of her parted lips and the dark tongue between them.

At last orders we stand up, walk to the entrance without speaking about where we're going and as I lead her to my flat through dim, echoing streets, she places a hand on the back of my neck, stroking the spot where my fade meets my skin. The soft, short hairs buckle beneath her fingertips and the goose-bumps that spring up across my shoulders make me shake her off — for a second.

We still haven't kissed by the time we reach my room. It's up three flights of stairs and the final one is so narrow that I stand guard beneath her in case she stumbles on her way up. She perches on the edge of my bed, hands in her lap, and I take a seat beside her. My bed is made up with fresh sheets — soft white, gentle — and as she goes to unbutton my shirt I slip beneath them, tugging them around my shoulders, not drunk enough not to care. Saying nothing, she peels the sheets back and continues in her task, using both hands to open my shirt and lift it above my head. I put two fingers in the waistband of her jeans, bringing her closer to me, bringing her tongue to mine.

The world has changed enough these past weeks that to try and conceive of what might happen in the next feels foolish. I can say with some certainty that I won't find myself back at Moth Club, getting drunk on G&Ts. I don't know if I will accept my appointment. If I accept it, I don't know if it will be a mistake.

Each night I marathon episodes of the *L Word* with my flatmates. The three of us, all single, moved in at the start of March. We scream silently, and sometimes loudly, whenever there's a sex scene between a couple with real chemistry. None of us knows when we'll next experience anything close to it.

But I have the time now, whether I like it or not, to hold two ideas in my mind: my body as it is and my body as it could be. And a third, more a hope than an idea: that feeling pleasure because of, and not in spite of, my body might one day not be a precious rare thing, but a given.

Peter Scalpello

kindness

when did i stop being kind to you, &
why did I do that?
                    I found you
on vauxhall bridge, screaming that
you were going to
                    jump.

                         clinging on
to you i could
                sense you were folding
        in on yourself like the
feelers of a mimosa plant when

        touched.

when did I stop being?

                         kind to you &
why did i?   do that
                         we passed on
the street as my brow crumpled
                              in
sight of you, two boys frowning at each
        other to express their desire.

 intentions on a periphery; to fuck
                         or fight.

when did i stop being fuck to you & why
did I fight that? i don't cope well

                                  with being
oppressed, You said. you remind me
of how not to be   a dominator.

                                              why
            did I stop being   kind to you? &
when? did i do that

                     I couldn't tell you the
last time i let a scab
              just heal by itself.

pass it on

i don't know who it was.

from the lapse in time, an interval which
defined, thus a lapse in also judgement,
i could speculate ~ a set of
clenching shoulders, freckled from burn ~

his inner things, angled in longing ~
the sting of your beard, abrasive unto
my grimacing cheek ~ a feeling
of presence, motion that declares he is there,
so then i am here, too.

no, i don't know who it was,

& yet i concede the relevance
of certainty, for are we not cumulative; a seed
surely provoked by proximity, so willingly
invaded, to receive quota of a shared grief?

reciprocal affliction made
unique, my cellular rivalry
has domesticated. i ponder you now,
faceless clone ~ baring mutual insignia,
how to each other we

remain unknown.

outed

sun rising   i didn't particularly   want to   but i let him
inside me   all flesh   & bone   &   appetite   adult bodies made
of childhood wounds   we   tried   we   trawled through netflix
to find one without   an outed abusive male   actor as protagonist
isn't possible   he said   text the dealer so   i hit 'hi da–   it
predicts   'hi daddy'   & my thumbs   stained sly from app use
are we   'DISCREET' ?   we take   drugs because it's fun   &
because   we can   he says   he thinks he likes cocaine too
much   & meth too   much   painkiller   never again   he says
he   thinks   he   likes   straight   men more   'cause that's who
traumatised   him   called him   sissy   says it didn't seem
to be a problem   when they   were fucking him   always asks
high   "am i a good boy?"   ask yourself   that   three ridges the
rim of his ear   an

ellipsis   a warning   ash   in his hair   dew under   his nose.

  you were a trance   song played through   dying   speakers
      broke   out   the box you were   left in   & i
        became   your new box   emptied   out   like pigeon shit
          pavement   constellations
          comments on porn   sites   disclose   abuse
        & responses are   like "that's hot"   like   prelude
              to a sneeze
          tragedies give people a pass   to behave horribly but
              i was not   committed to it   how would it
                feel to be touched
                      by grace

Elizabeth Lovatt

Skin Diary

Skin hunger: a neurological phenomenon whereby people who do not receive regular skin-on-skin contact have been shown to be more likely to experience depression, anxiety and insomnia.

26 MARCH

Hives appeared today on middle and index finger on back of right hand. Could be hay fever or could be eczema or could be too much hand washing or could be stress. Not itchy. Just little red bumps that most people probably wouldn't even notice.

Little finger on my left hand has a lump on it, only small and soft, where the crease is. Like a bunion on my finger. Maybe from resting my phone on it too much? Cyborg-ish. Tested it with my phone just now and the bump is just about where my little finger meets the base of the phone. I need to stop looking at Twitter.

27 MARCH

J thought she'd found a mole she'd never seen before on me, the one on my left elbow that always has a hair sticking out of it. I told her she'd definitely seen it before, but she reckons not. Two years together and there's still a bit of skin she hasn't felt before.

28 MARCH

When I woke this morning J kissed me on my shoulder, straight onto the skin and nuzzled her face into me, pressing her mouth close and wrapped her arm around me. I wanted to stay like that for a lot longer, but I knew she had to get up for work. She has to leave much earlier now because of the train times. It's strange that she leaves the house every day, her job being one of importance, while I stay home to stare at my laptop screen, connected to my colleagues each doing the same. Pockets of isolated individual offices that can't touch.

29 MARCH
Ripped off a strip of skin next to my right thumbnail this evening. J told me to stop so I did it under the blanket where she couldn't see. Had to use my teeth to sever it off properly which made a weird crunching sound.

30 MARCH
The tear on my thumb, where the tender flesh underneath was exposed has already started to harden over. The new skin is learning fast its role as barrier to the world.

31 MARCH
Picked a spot on my back. J told me to leave it as it wasn't ready (she was the one who found it) my fingers went instantly to the spot and scratched it off. It bled for ages, that bright red fresh kind of blood and J pressed a tissue to it a couple of times to stop it bleeding through onto my t-shirt. She showed me the tissue, *Look it's bleeding loads* and told me off for scratching it when she said not to.

1 APRIL
Hives still on my hand, but they don't itch. I want to scratch at them to make them sore because it would be something to do. I scratch, the skin breaks, it heals over. If you don't have any problems you can always make one and watch your body fix itself on your behalf. I never asked my skin to do this, but it does.

Maybe that's why I watch those videos of pimples being popped even though it makes me feel a little sick. It's like watching *Law and Order*, the pimple is popped, the bad guy is caught, everything gets wrapped up neatly by the end. We all come off clean.

2 APRIL

Hives on my hand are worse. Maybe after I'd been out and washed it with the washing up liquid instead of soap? Around my knuckles is the worst because they are swollen and hurt when I straighten my finger out, like the skin is stretched tight over those places. It reminds me of when I was younger and white yellowish spots appeared on my thumb and mum had to burst each one with a needle. I remember it hurt and I cried a lot but I got Milkybar Buttons afterwards. I want to gnaw at my knuckles, but I know it will hurt more and now I want Milkybar Buttons but we don't have any in the flat and I can't just pop to the shop to get some.

The insides of my arms are itchy as well but I'm doing better at ignoring that.

3 APRIL

Picked heel of my foot while on a one-and-a-half-hour work call. Little white flakes of dead skin fell into my lap as I did it and some bigger chunks came off which I piled onto the desk to clear away later.

By mid-afternoon hives on my right hand were much redder and stood out against my skin.

5 APRIL

Ripped the skin again from around my right thumb, bled a little but fine. Healing over already.

6 APRIL

Burnt my right arm this morning, between wrist and elbow on steam from the kettle. I was reaching for J's coffee measurer to make her coffee just after the kettle had boiled. Stupid really. Ran it under the tap for minute or so. It went red all over either from the burn or the cold water or both. Now the patch is smaller but skin still hot to the touch and stings. Put some Aloe Vera gel on it to try to get it to cool. J was running late and seemed annoyed that I'd burnt myself or maybe it was just the way I told her I did it. She gave me the gel though and told me to run it under the tap again. She thinks I don't take care of myself.

7 APRIL
Picked a spot on my jawline that bled and bled. Put a piece of tissue on it and forgot it was there so it dried to my face. When I took it off a bit of the dried blood came off too. It was bright red still, a little cap made of spot juice and blood. It looks like a tiny garnet shining in the sun.

9 APRIL
Small cut on the back of my left hand has appeared. I don't remember doing it. More like a scratch really.

10 APRIL
Fingertip eczema on my left little finger and ring finger is back. It's been a year or so since I last had it like this, little criss-crossing lines that run over my fingerprints and crack the skin. There's a dry patch at the centre of each pad. I show it to J, but she says she can't really see anything.

11 APRIL
A quiet day so plenty to pick at.

13 APRIL
Mole on my face was sore today, scratched at it a little and it felt swollen like there was a spot behind but nothing came out. It does this sometimes.

Once I saw a woman in the street with her mole on her face

and I thought *why doesn't she get that lasered off?* before remembering that I have a mole on my face that I would never think of removing because it's part of my face. Felt bad at the time.

15 APRIL
Just before bedtime accidently knocked my mole when blowing my nose and blood started pouring out right away. Bled for a long while but stuck a tissue on it until it stopped.

18 APRIL
J asked me to help squeeze a blackhead underneath her armpit that she says has been there for years and every now and then fills up with gunk that needs extracting. She told me to pinch the skin as hard as I could, but the angle was difficult and her skin so soft there that my fingers just sunk into her without getting any purchase. She told me to pinch harder and I did but then she exclaimed not to use my nails since that hurt. I couldn't do it in the end, so she squeezed it herself and a thick white burst of gunk came out, only a few millimetres long with some more trailing out after it. She told me to squeeze it some more, so I did but only succeeded in getting a little more out.

We have always done this, picked and squeezed at each other. J is always carefully picking hairs or bits of dry skin off my face that I can't see. She offers up spots for me to squeeze and I ask her to tweezer out the sporadic black hairs under my chin that appear without warning. It makes me think of nature documentaries where chimps groom fleas off one another or remora fish who attach themselves to sharks thousands of times larger than themselves, living off the shark's dead skin and their own usefulness. Symbiotic relationships, David Attenborough knowingly describes it in voiceovers.

19 APRIL
Don't you think it's weird that you're the only other person I'll touch for weeks? I ask J. She shrugs and doesn't reply.

20 APRIL

The eczema on my fingers continues to be dry and patchy, spreading from the pads of my ring and little finger to the edge of my middle finger. Doesn't itch unless I think about it.

21 APRIL

Went out for a walk after several days inside. Sunlight is supposed to be good for eczema. I could feel my fingertips itching as I walked. The skin is rough to the touch.

23 APRIL

Woke up with red welts on my arm, five of them in long parallel lines leading from the crook of my elbow down towards my wrist. I must have scratched at my arm in the early hours but I don't remember doing it. Placed my fingers over the welts to line up my nails and they did, except there was one extra line so I must have done it more than once.

24 APRIL

The mole on my face has finally healed over and looks as it did before.

25 APRIL

I've noticed that the first thing we do when we wake is move closer to each other from where we have drifted apart in the night. One of us will reach out a hand and lay it on a piece of bare skin, an arm, a thigh, the soft round of a hip. The lightest of touches. The easiest way to say *I am here with you.*

Saurabh Sharma

So how does it feel?

These days I dream of visiting Connaught Place, 9 km from northeast Delhi, where I live. Always bustling with queerness, so many of us giving a different colour, a different texture to this part of the city. In Connaught Place, a guy's hand grazes over his crotch, looking at me. Someone in heels, struggling to walk, might ask a friend to wait for them. Someone will adjust their look in a mirror, priming their makeup, while next to them someone checks out Grindr hoping for a quickie. A person on the opposite side of the road is lured to the public washroom with a look. Some remain seated in front of the A Block Starbucks, looking for customers as an old artist draws portraits, to please himself or sometimes by request. Other people are just there, just celebrating, just being themselves.

On March 24, 2020, the Prime Minister of India announced a nationwide lockdown to try and curb the spread of a virus that was killing people across the globe. We had known about this virus since December 2019, but Trump was visiting, and the Delhi State Elections had yet to pass. When the COVID-19 lockdown was announced three months later, it wasn't the first time I had heard this term. On August 5, 2019, the Indian government announced it would be locking down Kashmir, and that all communication with the (erstwhile) state of Jammu & Kashmir would be cut off. Only a few understood what it meant. Only those who have been isolated, bullied and discriminated against by the State machinery felt the pain of the Kashmiris.

And now here was the term again: Lockdown. This time, the whole nation has just four-hours' notice from the PM. As public transport shuts down, we watch migrant workers and their families walk barefoot, hundreds of kilometres, trying to get to their hometowns and villages. Some die on the way. Some are beaten for flouting the rules. While 'educated' people start hoarding essential food items like chocolates, Maggi packets, and posting their home workouts and dinners on Instagram, no one pays attention to either the poorest nor a population of over 100 million people — 8% of India's population — the queer community.

Due to the structural flaws in our society and labour laws, some of us are worst hit by the pandemic. Some of us aren't even citizens, some only partially. India decriminalised homosexuality in September 2018, but in August the following year, on the same day they locked down Kashmir, India also snatched away the rights of trans people by passing the ironically-named Transgender Persons (Protection of Rights) Bill, which was instrumental in stripping away their rights. Many trans folx don't have their names registered on government social welfare schemes to provide the (meagre) sum of 500 rupees (about £5) because they don't even have Aadhaar, one of the identity cards needed to register for the welfare schemes.

With little to no paraphernalia to sustain them, the problem is more pernicious for the indigenous Indian queer population: the Hijras, the Kothis, the Aravanis, the Jogappas and others. *Where do they go now to earn a living?* Their own family members often don't want them. For many, the means to earn a livelihood is sex work — impossible during this time.

What's most difficult to bear for many is not the (non) intervention of the State laws and regulations, but the immediate autocracy at home, the rule of our families. It's difficult to remain quarantined under the constant vigilance of our homophobic, misogynistic and patriarchal parents. And those who've no family are facing worse. Many organisations are reaching out to people online to help and support the queer community. But social distancing to flatten the curve is, in essence, slimming our chances to survive.

When I began working from home, I was asked: "So how does it feel?" The accompanying snort was, of course, a snide remark on my daily socialising (read: hookups), on my queerness — on my community's mobility, our mindless pursuit to find the next catch. Skepticism toward relationships haunts us: we've been betrayed too often by our partners, who won't or can't come out, who give in to the parental demands for a straight marriage. We have neither protection from the State nor full citizenry — how do you want us to exercise our queerness in full measure? We've reduced it to a common denominator: sex. And I guess most of us are fine with that.

We, who are always on the move, now face restrictions on our movement. That intimacy — the desire to be loved, to be laid, to walk together hand in hand with our full makeup on — is what I miss most. But we will survive this. We are still united against our common, shared experience of rejection, hatred, and ostracism. And united in our humour: we could say that the coronavirus is the rain. And that it's raining, as they say, like cats and dogs. We might as well take our *chattris** with us whenever we go out.

*umbrellas, an Indian slang for condoms.

Sam J Grudgings

Welcome Home Lonely Skin

Early bedtimes adopt the wary
who in turn adopt the haunted look
of government sanctioned internalised
phobias, about adult things such as
answering phone calls, remembering
to tell your mother you love her, cooking
meals for yourself, not as an act of
self care but of necessity, closing doors
behind you, burying the dead.

To whom it may concern, it mustn't
don't let this destroy you, unmake you,
tear you from the foundations of today
I have observed the wound in home
from having left it. I scar like scaffolding
even knowing I will return. You are a ghost
sick of your own staying. In a world of leaving,
being haunted is a kindness.

Salt settles in wounds and there seem to be
more mornings than last nights. It hurts.
Skin is not rationed, not turning into evenings,
being away is the high cost of salvation.
Sanctuary can look a lot like an unmade bed
undo the sleeplessness you are preventing
covet your touch, it is the most human thing,
you are prevented from doing

that defines you upon returning.

Netflix and Chill
Only Make it Existential

If anyone wants to span the gaps
between my ribs, the bone and breath where capture is
absent, to find
failure's contortionism, to count

each protrusion like it's their own,
you are welcome. It will mean I don't have to
trap fingers in the bars
of cages I keep my heart in, I have had enough
          of searching for proof that I am living. In my skin
excuses have no room to be.

Doubt's line of questioning seldom makes
for satisfying responses.
My body,
          in this way, is evidence
          of caution,
my body,
          in this way, is,
          if not a crime scene,
                    then at least a suspect.

Superlatives heal slowest.
That's been true   since day one
in the spaces between punches
either exchanged   or delivered, there is only

a void. In this way we are all guilty
of looking for responses, or answers,

or redemption, in the lives of others. Ignorance
adores a vacuum.

Some wounds have no border patrols
and the divorce   of skin
from muscle   has left an open ended request
 to corroborate   your version of events.

This is not intended
as an indictment for searching
          but the meat of answers
does not sustain the violence of looking.

Prove me innocent,
the cold case,   of my body
and guilty verdicts fall apart
Uncover, some tentative archaeology
of what I was
prove that my life, delicate still lingers

Cleo Henry

I Miss You, Robert Mapplethorpe

If I had known how to tell this story, I would have told it sooner. But as it is I told it late and badly.

It's not even a story, just a truth. One of those truths that you start to say off-hand like you say dozens of things a day, maybe hundreds, I don't know who you are or how many people you talk to a day but for me it's probably dozens of things. Maybe fifty on a big day with a lunch or a dinner. So maybe you are at one of those lunches or dinners, which I was, and you start to say a sentence like you say others. You are a person full of sentences; you have done things and seen things and you can describe them. But in the middle of this one, when the first few words have trotted out like everything's normal, you realise that it's true. Not that the others were lies. But this one is truer and closer and comes from just under your sternum and everyone in the room can tell, can see all the blood on it. It is like you are showing them photos of your baby, just born, and they say it's beautiful even though it's blue and screaming and covered in stuff they don't understand. And that's how this truth came out, all blue and screaming, and I didn't know until the middle.

I am at this lunch because a girl dropped a bag of oranges in the fresh produce aisle. They spilled out around her feet and it was highly embarrassing for her. When she caught my eye as I helped gather them from the floor, a small projector flickered on for both of us and showed us both the same film. It was us right then, the gleam of the bright oranges on the speckled white lino. Then it was holding hands on weathered promenades, cooking terrible food together with our heads back laughing, bickering in the car as we miss our junction, all that stuff, and we both saw the exact same things at the exact same time. She had a small scar on her forehead in the shape of the constellation Ursa Major and I told her this. I said The scar on your forehead is the shape of Ursa Major and she said Come to this lunch with me.

So I'm at this lunch and a man I only met twenty minutes ago asks if we had imaginary friends growing up. We had a few giant ponies, a few kids called Joe. Tantrums, appeals, the eventual loss. Then there it was, the crack in my chest and my bones are open and I'm sicking truth up all over the chequered tablecloth. It's so distasteful.

When I was fourteen till I was sixteen, my best friend was Robert Mapplethorpe.

They are holding the baby and they know it's special and the wonder of life but oh my god what is all this stuff. They are smiling because they are polite people. I realise I have literally never said that out loud, never at all, to anyone and suddenly I am the loneliest person in North London.

Before Robert, I would watch Katie Mortiz in my class. She had a cross around her neck and I would watch her touch it before tests, when we stood to eat, when we sat back down. It was like a circuit that for tiny moments came together and what had been loose and useless was whole and lit up. I thought of the gold chain snapping in my hands as I took it. But I was never one of those kids who stole and we were allowed to take reasonably sized lucky charms into exams, so I tried that.

Keychains, shells, figurines. A small cat with beaded eyes. A spider suspended like a devastating rupture in a piece of amber. Marbles like milky eyes. The detritus from a child's life, all kept. It pooled in my pockets, at the bottom of bags. My clothes bulged with them, a plasticy, rattling layer between my body and all the choices it made and the places it had to be. I was all water, all sloppy and I clattered with talismans as I walked.

When I saw him, they fell from me like a shedded skin.

A coffee table book on New York photographers and there he was. He was the Angel Gabriel walked into a saloon bar, curls and faded Americana. And with him came men in leather, kneeling in front of each other openchested. With him was cock piercings and hooped collars. The hills of Derbyshire lapped at my window, craning to glimpse a studded, boyishness I half recognised from somewhere in the middle of me. And that was it, he was cuffed about my neck, the doe faced albatross of a queer tragedy I didn't know I had been longing for.

Mostly all we did together was leave and arrive. The back of my head bobbing towards his car as he pulled up to the curb. I would get in and he would say Hey and I would say Hey then we would drive away, towards things and places I couldn't picture yet.

He waited on thresholds, leant against doorframes. He would be standing by baggage claim, a halo of golden light against the coldness of airport terminal bulbs. He would know which bag was mine and have a sign with my name on it and there would be no traffic getting home. He was empty roads and punctual trains. He would cross streets towards me and I towards him and each time we knew that we were young and beautiful and this short journey towards each other was momentous and arrival was the discovery of a new planet altogether, verdant and dangerous.

I would walk into rooms again and again, and he would stand again and again, rising from the hum of people sitting on the floor and raise his hand at me. The light would catch in his curls and he would look like the pub at the edge of a sleeping village, ablaze and alive.

Robert never photographed me. He never even had a camera on him. What we had was not made for posterity. It was a love stuffed into transitions, all the blood and pulse of it in the second the ice skate clicks back on the ice and not the jump. You can't photograph that click without making it a moment. I didn't want scenes or set pieces, just the feeling of going from room to room and he would be in both, calling "This room was waiting for your body to be in it!"

I suppose it's right, then, that there wasn't a final time. One day, he must have driven off and not come back, or stood up, arm raised, and it was the last time, just like that, and I never even noticed until right now, at this lunch. I try now to imagine him as a lover leaving. On a train platform, maybe, mist billowing at his feet as I lean from the carriage waving a white handkerchief, all surrender. Or like Euridice, falling backwards into some betrayed darkness, palm up and open like a flower blazing against the underworld. But I can't. He is already too far away.

I am standing over the ruin of this lunch party. I will never be invited back. Giant doors are being slammed in my face but for a second all there is is the power of ruining something. I have ruined a perfectly nice time and I stamp on its smouldering remains. I look down at my body and I am head to toe leather. It holds my torso tightly like a warm fist, keeping me in and whole. I am straps and buckles entirely. I am holding a whip in one hand and a crucifix in the other. No wonder they are staring, pale and moonlike, as if I am telling them the worst piece of news they will ever hear in their lives. I am the doorman of some great change.

Tears are stinging the eyes of the girl who brought me here. When she had seen my hand stop the roll of her oranges, she hadn't known it was attached to a leather bound harbinger of a new species. I hadn't, either. These were her friends. You couldn't blame her frustration. In another world, there could have been a compromise. She could have playfully snapped the tautness of my harness as we joke over smoothies. We could have fed the ducks as the chain that connects my neck to the leash she holds sparkles in the setting sun. But that was another world.

I want to tell her this, and tell her that I was not cut out for montages. I am a person who sits in the transitions, and, in a way, that's because of Robert.

What I could have told her, though, was that I miss you, Robert Mapplethorpe. I enter rooms just fine and there are people there who like me just fine. But to stand as you did, half up half down, that moment of acknowledgement. That is a form of grace to me and when I miss it I feel like the universe is huge and cold and I am small, the last heat source after the apocalypse, getting colder.

Erica Gillingham

The Gallery Floor

On days when we'd go to the galleries,
I chose my shoes based on their sound
against the concrete or hardwood floors.
Smart yet quiet, I wanted the day's rhythm
punctuated by our companionate shuffle,
overlaid by the chatter of the patrons
and our cheeky side remarks. Spoken
in hushed tones during the intersection
of our orbits, we'd reveal which pictures
would hang in our homes, if possible,
ones that left us besotted, and those
we just couldn't care less about—
a statement typically followed by a nod
and an exit into the next exhibition room.
We spent time together elsewhere, too,
but, in the galleries, our edges became soft,
our bodies, like birds, finding the upwash,
a lifting only possible with proximity,
my feet barely brushing the floor.

When We Fuck With Our Fingers

When we fuck with our fingers / it's like driving a manual transmission
headed west on a far-flung deserted highway / with the windows
rolled down to let in the heat, the breeze / your hand upon my thigh
and nowhere we have to be / but right here: the radio humming,
the thrum of our bodies / hurtling toward the horizon line and an endless sky.

When we fuck with our fingers / we are exploring *terra incognita*,
traversing the hills, the valleys, the ravines / reading the contours
for a route through the wilderness / with only each other for company
and an unquenchable thirst / until, maybe, just maybe, we crest the peak
of the continental divide / and find our way home, again.

When we fuck with our fingers / it's like scanning the lines of poetry
finding the rhythms of iambs with our fingertips / the delight
in the breaks of this phenomenal woman / with her slant rhymes
and hive of honey bees / the rapture of repetition, repetition, repetition
offering a release of so many words / we can no longer hold onto.

When we fuck with our fingers / we are conducting an orchestra
in the finest concert halls of Europe / arranging the strings, the bass,
the breath, the timpani, from lento to crescendo / we know the melody,
we have rehearsed for days, months, years / each iteration begs
a fresh ear, the plush seats / the acoustics of the new day.

When we fuck with our fingers / it's like diving from the deck
into the dark, brackish, fathomless sea / the exhilarating chill
tingling across exposed skin / the catch of the lungs and
an all-consuming freedom / of limbs and bellies and breasts
the lingering salt in the palm of my hand / long after the waves have subsided.

Gabrielle Johnson

Cold Feet, Warm Hands

You know that song lyric 'you held onto me like a crucifix'? My dad used to play that song in his van when he was driving and tilt his chin up just a little when that lyric came up, tapping his nails against the dashboard real hard so they make a clicking sound in time with the music. I always thought it must hurt but I think his nails had probably hardened from all the times he'd hit them instead of the nail he was aiming for on some roof. That lyric though, I think about it every time we're fucking, in those moments when I put my whole body on top of yours and imagine that every inch of our skin is touching. I think of that lyric when you wrap your arms around my back and lock your fingers together, pressing me hard against you; I never feel better than when we're like that. Maybe because it makes me forget my body or maybe because it feels like you need me, and maybe you wouldn't be able to survive without me. It's sick but I fucking love it, makes the sex even better. When we're done and you ask why I'm quiet, it's usually because I'm coming to, realising that probably one day you won't need me.

Sometimes I look at pictures of celebrities who used to date looking super happy and wonder whether I'll look back at photos of us like that. I seek them out, those '10 celebrities you didn't know used to be together' bait stories. When everyone else at work is on WhatsApp web I'm two pages deep into Google photos and on bad days, scrolling Tumblr like some thirteen year-old with too many feelings, looking at photos of when x and x were together and in love and at this restaurant or this event or if I'm really lucky, at home doing something me and you do. It helps when they're musicians cause I can plug in and listen to one of their break-up songs at the same time, wonder if they wrote it about their ex, wonder if I should learn an instrument so I can write something for you once we're done. I see everything as if it's ending I guess, but sometimes that makes it sweeter.

Yesterday I walked past three people I knew you'd like to fuck. I made a list in the notes on my phone so I could stop thinking about them:

1. This dude with long legs and straight black trousers that bit at his ankles. He was wearing that kind of hat you told me I should get months ago that I never did. He didn't have one with him but you could tell he owned a skateboard.
2. This big butch ordering a coffee in front of me at Starbucks, black iced, heavy shit. She looked like the woman in that gay TV show I made you watch: 'she's not hot but I'm attracted to her' that's what you said.
3. In all fairness the last person was so hot I wanted her too, or maybe I wanted her cause I knew you would. Her head was shaved to like one centimeter long but dyed blond so you could barely see it. She smiled at me when she saw me looking and I wouldn't even blame you if you wanted her more than me.

I see people who you would like the whole time and I think about you fucking them, them fucking you the way I do it. Sometimes it turns me on but most of the time it just makes that spot above my ass tingle like when you're young and you wake in the night because it feels like someone's in your room.

⬧

Last night I matched with someone on hinge and it was late and I'd already had three drinks with my flatmates so I met them at the pub next to my house. When I got there they were waiting outside the door of the place in the cold like they needed my permission to enter. They were taller than me which usually puts me off but they looked like someone you might like and that made me feel like I was walking down the street next to you so I bought them a drink. Their personality wasn't like mine or anyone you'd be into but I said they could come over to my place because it was close and I wanted another drink but not at those prices. We went straight upstairs at mine because I was already on thin ice with my flatmates for being such an ass since me and you ended. It probably looked like a move but I honestly just didn't want to piss my flat off and I was tired and wanted to get it over with so they would leave and I could go back to thinking of ways to stop thinking about you.

They sat on my bed and smoked out of my window without checking first, which I thought was rude but not worth mentioning. I sat on the bed waiting for them to finish. I didn't want to just stare at them while they smoked but they weren't speaking because their head was halfway out the window, so I just looked at my wall. There's usually three little drawings in a row on it that my sister did at school before she passed, but one has fallen down onto the shelf underneath, it's been there for weeks now. I've been in and out of the house, I've watered the plants that are next to the drawings, but I haven't picked it back up and put it back on the wall. The other two are too far from each other now.

They asked me to choose a safe word so I chose the word we used to use, and thought about what you'd say if you knew I'd done that. It made fucking them better than I'd expected.

You always wake on your back after falling asleep on your side. I say wake but it takes a while, I can usually get half an hour's worth of stuff done before you are awake enough to hold a conversation, and even then you talk with your eyes closed, semi-conscious. You say I taste the best when I kiss you in the mornings, the way you open your mouth and inhale. 'Worst and best' you say.

'You were talking again last night'

'Oh yeah? What about'

'I can't remember now', you roll into my neck and pull your knees to your belly.

'Scratchcard'

'Huh?'

'I can't remember what you were saying but I had a dream we bought a scratchcard and won. Let's do that today'.

We spent the day at the lido in Tooting Bec, the one that's always in the magazines people leave on the tube. You'd wanted to go for ages because you missed the sea and this was the closest we could get. You had on one of those black swimsuits that women always wear in old movies that are really high at the front but low at the back. The way you waved at me from the water made me want to learn to swim.

We bought a scratchcard on our way home, from an off licence that stank like cat piss and sold poppers in a glass counter. The guy asked you which one you wanted but of course you'd never bought one before so you asked me to choose. I picked the one with the highest number printed in some font that looked like comic sans but worse. 'Let's wait until we're home to see if we've won' you said.

You had to scratch three areas off to find out if you'd won. We needed three pictures of coins, or one picture of coins and two of money bags, or something like that. I flipped off my phone case and we used the sharpest corner to scratch the grey coating off, going at it like an old dude with a metal detector digging in the mud. Instead of money bags there was a picture of some cherries, two red fruits dangling there taunting you. You put the card on the side and went into the kitchen.

◗

After we finished I didn't let them stay but my sheets smelt like sex and cum and something that isn't me or you. Most mornings now I wake up sweating. I had the same dream again last night that I keep on having, it's the day that we bought the scratchcard but instead of you waking up from a dream of us buying one and winning, you dream that we break up, and we spend our day trying to buy some sort of resolution to our problems in offies and from strangers on the street. Every time we walk into a shop you run to a glass counter and scan the aisles of poppers, asking the guy to double-check in case he doesn't realise he's restocked. You said in your dream we worked it out: we found the resolution and we went home and scratched the surface of our own skin until we started bleeding the answers and could create some sort of future that worked. 'Let's just keep on looking' you say in my dream, but I always wake up before we find anything.

My flatmates made me delete all of the photos we took together, so I can't look at them while I'm working, but sometimes I still look at pictures of the celebrities. A couple of them have got back together now.

Helen Savage

The Matter

Looking after the matter so that any member of the public who can prove ID and a home address can borrow it. If he matters enough – that's if he has a permanent address – he is entitled to borrow 15 items in one go and he can renew them indefinitely. If he does not matter enough he will have restrictions on the amount of matter he can borrow and for how long. If he matters enough he is entitled to lots of matter. If he doesn't really matter and can only show a temporary address or no address or only has unofficial ID or no ID then he can not have much matter and that is how it works here. Looking after the public matter by ensuring that it has been entered correctly on the computer system, by checking that it has all the correct barcodes and identity papers inside to tell us where it belongs. If the matter comes apart due to wear or tear or looks as if it might begin to deteriorate due to unknown and outside forces using special tape. Opening the matter now at its seam and placing the tape along its spine to hold it together. Putting the matter on its self, shelving. Lifting the public matter. Sometimes the matter is heavy so bending the legs to pick up the matter and taking it easy whilst walking with the matter across the space. The workers who do this work care for all the matter. For what is good and what is bad and, such, their stance is outside of 'taste'. Outside of the stylish city, on the edges, at the fringes: belief. They work for a public service and they will care for the matter in public ownership. That is until the worker is handed a gimmick. A gimmick's favourite game is to mock the public but they forget that they mock the worker too. A gimmick has nothing to do with real matter; with dirt and mud and soil and moss and bark and water. A gimmick is a book that is against nature; is against the warming climate. A gimmick makes a mockery of the workers attention, makes a mockery out of the time spent in the office, and makes a mockery of the workers hands. An example of a gimmick includes *Theory of the Gimmick: Aesthetic Judgment and Capitalist Form.*

The matter is that the workers have low morale the workers do not have team meetings. Sometimes the matter goes missing. The material goes missing, the object goes missing and the workers mark it on the computer system as just that, missing. It is often a problem when something is missing and this is the case for the workers. For the workers what is missing is support, is a pay-rise, and this is the matter. What is missing is a Christmas party, is a team meeting. Is recognition of their work, is opportunity for progress. Is a 'well done' from a fellow colleague, is a team meeting. The matter is that the workers are unsatisfied by their repetitive and physically straining work. The matter is that the workers' work is not engaging, it's that they get distracted easily. The matter is that because of this when one of the workers hands touches another of the workers hands when passing over the matter, it feels mildly erotic and this is so unusual it sends them into a state of shock for 3 days. The workers are not used to being touched. Not by their work, not by their colleagues. Not by their lovers because they are always in a rush to get back to work. Their work or the object of their work does not touch the workers and this is what the problem is: the matter they are handling does not matter to the worker. The workers can order in matter that does matter to them. They aren't given the time to pour over it. The matter is that the workers are not able to read fantasy fiction, or fiction. The matter is that the workers do not have the time or inclination to read. The matter is that there is no one in the position to say 'well done'. The person who used to say this has been erased from the workplace. Those words, erased from the memories of the workers, erased from the face of the earth. All the workers are left with is to fantasize about it inside their own heads. The workers make up scenarios in their heads in which the words 'well done' are uttered. How elaborate these fantasies are depends on how the workers are feeling that day. In one such fantasy all the workers stand without any clothes on holding placards which read 'well done Sue', all desiring the worker and bowing down to her.

Adam Zmith

Armpit

I have been wondering if I could move in. Move in to your armpit, I mean. Could I live here? Would you have me? If I was small enough I could live in your armpit. I would like to live with you, Ammar, if you would have me. I think your armpit would be a lovely place to live. Better than Grimsby, which my mum says is the "arsehole of nowhere". Your arsehole is lovely too. It is as warm as your armpit, and just as hairy. But I am not suggesting I live in your arsehole even though it is, of course, an *arsehole of somewhere*. No, I'm looking into your armpit, mmmm it feels so warm. Your armpit is where I am asking to live. I think it's time I moved in.

Ammar lets me finish, but he does not wait too long to speak. He knows that if he pauses for long I will remake my case for living in his armpit. I take a sniff there as he starts to talk. I want his smell to spread inside my body while I listen to him. I lay my hand among the hairs on his chest too. It moves with his breathing, and I like to feel it. He strokes my head, as a father touches a baby he is sending to sleep. Words come. At first his words tumble into a chuckle. He is stunned, he is amused, he grips me a little tighter, and says yes. He says yes, it is time for me to move in.

We need to figure out whether I am moving in as a tenant or what. And of course I need to shrink small enough. Ammar, I want to let you know that I intend to keep the place clean and tidy. Oh, but I like your armpit when it is not too clean. This is how I have always liked men's armpits. The scent of your salty dark cubby, right here, is too magnificent to wash away. It gives me a high when I breathe it in, better than the marker pens we used to sniff at school. So it is going to be difficult to decide between my good housekeeping and my wish to keep your armpit the way I like it.

Investigating how on earth I can be shrunk down to fit into Ammar's armpit is a challenge. I have never had much to do with the medical establishment beyond vaccinations and sexual health checkups. My arm broke when I was a kid, and after a day of practising the story my mum let me go to the hospital. But broken arms are easier then wanting to be shrunk. Google searches turn up nothing. The NHS website has pages on dwarfism and gastric bands for weight loss, but not how to be shrunk. Even though it is to do with my body, it is not really a medical issue. But now my Googling has stopped because the internet has stopped.

I will be so cosy when I live inside your armpit. I will snuggle down into my bed made from your soft hairs and I will be surrounded by all of the rest of you.

I refresh my pages and my feeds for ten minutes. All dead. My messages from Ammar stop too. I lay out on my bed, and think that I would not need my devices if Ammar was here for a hug. I need to find out what is happening with the internet but I am trying to avoid my landlord. I can hear him laughing at the television in the living room where I never spend any time anymore. The stand-up comedian's sermon gets angrier and louder as I slide off my bed and out into the living room. "I closed the account," Tony says, without taking his eyes away from the glowing screen. "Not worth paying for an extra month when we're moving out this weekend."

I am drawn to living in you because I do not like to take up space. Tony said my pile of shoes blocked the hallway. He said my Cokes in the fridge were bigger than his beers and cheese and jars. He said I am at home a lot. So I have to tell you now

that when I move into your armpit I will be there all the time. It should not be surprising really, given the circumstances. But I wanted to warn you that I'll be taking up the smallest amount of space I can, in the world, and in your armpit. Does that sound OK?

Ammar says he knows I can do anything I set my mind to. If people can do terrible things, he says, they can also do wonderful things. So I look beyond the NHS. Most people do not understand how small I need to get. They think all I want is a tummy tuck or liposuction. A guy in the warehouse says I should try his gym. He lost two stone and now he needs new jeans.

We do not have much time to get our lives sorted, and I want you to know that I am trying hard. I would not want you to jeopardise your place, or to scare the government or the woman from the charity. That is why I will be small. No one will know that I'm living in your armpit, Ammar. Just think about it. We will spend all our time together. I will leave my job because I won't need to earn any money. I won't need to buy clothes or food. I will nibble on your scraps. I know I will be satisfied with the corner of your chip and a little smudge of banana.

I pay more attention to adverts during these final days before the new owners of Tony's flat move in. I see posters advertising heat sprays for my sports injuries, apps to help me invest in stocks and shares, companies that will send boxes of food to me. Even in the television ads, which have a bigger budget, there is nothing advertised to help a person with shrinking. All I want is a way to be smaller.

You won't charge me rent, will you? Relax! I know you wouldn't do that. It makes me laugh how you look as stern as a soldier when I wind you up.

My mum would describe the woman I found as a "freak". But pioneers are often weird, and my mum hates everyone. Josephine's arms are a circus of tattoos, all colours and characters. She hugs me with them in her dad's ice-cream van. Her face is untouched. No tattoos and no make-up. Her eyes are as clear and bright as a sunny day. Her dad has mostly retired now, so Josephine is using the van more and more for her own business because the freezers are useful during the shrinking. I decide not to tell Josephine about my housing situation, about my plan of where to live. Ammar is used to keeping a low profile.

Josephine tells me how she invented her method with some help from the engineering department at the Grimsby Institute. "Not the biology department?" I ask. Josephine smiles and says that's where so many people had gone wrong previously. This is when I know I've found a genius.

The plan is our plan, Ammar. No one else needs to know.

Josephine has helped so many people already, but that does not mean she would understand if I say I want to move into a man's armpit. I could tell her that I've already moved five times in the past three years due to landlords selling up, or housemates being dickheads, or rent rises, and that all this was what made me want to find a way to take up less space. I like being small. I think it's because I used to curl up in the corner in my bedroom after Mum moved all her extra stuff in and began to call it the spare room. I left when she stopped sharing food with me.

No one will really understand what we mean to each other. How could they possibly comprehend what it was like for you to live underground, to see your town destroyed, to flee? How could they understand what it feels like for me to find someone who I want to be inside? No one will understand you and me, Ammar.

Ammar comes from a town on the banks of the Euphrates River, which is creamy and green. The water used to look like the milky melted insides of a mint Aero chocolate bar. But the river was gross by the time Ammar left, junked with rubble and landfill and the dead bodies of people he knew. I know my plan sounds as impossible as Ammar's escape. I am his first boyfriend, and he is mine—so everything seems impossible. But we are moving. Ammar and I are giddy with momentum. It feels like we are surging down a milky green river into the future.

Ammar, if I can be evicted five times in three years, if landlords can sell their flats from under my feet, if flatmates can be so awful, so filthy, if I have to double my travel time with the bus because the train is too expensive, if you can see your school bombed, if you can lose your parents and your brother, if the government here needs to hold you in this situation, if we cannot plan anything—then maybe we can never have somewhere to live.

But if we can find each other, if I can taste your scent in the back of my throat, and if you can let your body relax when I alone hold you—then maybe anything is possible.

All I am trying to do is move in to your armpit. This is how I can be inside you. It is how we can be together no matter what decision the Home Office makes tomorrow.

People say that it is important to have somewhere to call your own. You can change the wallpaper and things like that. But I have never cared about wallpaper and things like that. I think it's OK to rent, except when the rate goes up or when the flatmates are filthy. Or except when you can't go out anymore so it's important to feel safe and secure at home.

The thing is, I am like Ammar. I just want to be safe. On the first day we met he said he could tell that I had escaped something too, just like him. We spoke all night that night, with static between us. It was a tangible feeling of something shared. I had escaped something different to what he had, but we realised how similar were our upbringings, our families. We wouldn't mind not to go out anymore, if we were safe inside each other somehow.

I'm ready for today's procedure, Ammar. I've never been more ready for anything. Josephine texted to say the conditions are perfect, and she got the backup generator she needed for the van.

I've been wondering: once I've moved in, maybe you could do it too. Ammar, I know. I know it sounds crazy, but it could work, couldn't it? I want you to be happy and safe. I'll give you Josephine's number. I am sure there is someone else who would like you to move into their armpit. I would not know the difference, if I am shrunk along with you at the same rate. I would be even smaller. I would be as small as an aphid in amber, locked in but safe forever.

Georgie Henley

Midtown

I hate the humidity but
when you put your hand on the back
of my neck I am saved a little,
it's not that your hand is cool
in fact it is too hot and damp
but I like the moments when you
touch me softly and unprompted
and sometimes, when I think
you are withdrawing entirely
you surprise me at the last second
like when we were walking
through crowded Midtown dusk
to get the tacos you like
and you reached out your hand behind you
hoping I would take it

Vita

it's midnight and I want
to be touched so bad that I fill up the bath
and pretend the water is made of hands

Annie Dobson

The Bed Essay

In Sarah Louise Baker's *Pop in(to) the Bedroom: Popular Music in Pre-Teen Girl's Bedrooms,* she writes that girls were *limited in their use of public space, or 'the street', which was viewed as the prime site of male consumption, and therefore the girls turned to domestic space, specifically the bedroom, to carry out their cultural activities.*

I have never gotten over the teenage intimacy of bedrooms. I do not consider myself to be close to anyone I have not cried in bed with. Sometimes I think of my life in bedrooms, all the beds I have put my body.

Miami's Bed: In the queer, teen film pastiche, *So Long Suburbia* (2016), the girls gather in Miami's bed after she is dumped by her emo boyfriend for being *too much of a teenybopper.*

> *Teenybop, the derogatory term given to music listened to by young girls, has become synonymous with triviality. Used to highlight the division between the young female pop music audience and the seriousness of male (youth) rock culture, teenybop has historically been either disregarded or ridiculed.[1]*

The pouty, hyper femme-ness of the character Miami, cartoony mascara running down her cheeks, pigtails, the fluffy, lilac top – campy nostalgia for the crying heroines of noughties teen films, *the relation of Camp taste to the past is extremely sentimental[2].* There

1   Baker, Sarah Louise. *Pop in(to) the Bedroom: Popular Music in Pre-Teen Girl's Bedrooms*

2   Sontag, Susan. *Notes on Camp*

is a ridiculousness, an extravagance of emotion & it is taken extremely seriously by everyone in the bed.

Miami is a bisexual trans girl & her friendship group is made up almost entirely of other queer teenagers. Miami's bedroom, surrounded by other queer women, is the safe place.

In a moment of realisation about her breakup, Miami delivers a monologue about her love of popular culture, ending with:

> *If someone thinks that pop music is any less meaningful or intelligent than metal or jazz, I don't want them in my life. If someone thinks that arthouse cinema is any more of a genius work of art than teen films, then they can go fuck themselves.*

The scene ends with the three other girls group-hugging Miami, a collective rejoicing.

(**My Bed:** There is a lot to be said for the second queer adolescence. *Nostalgia assumes its full meaning when the real is no longer what it was.*[3] The teenage intimacies of sleepovers are re-created in our early twenties, watching *But I'm A Cheerleader* in bed together because it was projected onto the wall at a DSFL club nite. I hope these platonic, bed-intimacies do not disappear when I am thirty, forty.)

Bed is a place of emotion. Bed is a place emotion is allowed – fully, extravagantly. Bed is a place to be decadent with our emotion, safe in the space bed allows, safe in the presence of the friends we are close enough with to share a bed.

When watching this scene in *So Long Suburbia,* I am reminded of the communal, female scream in *Midsommar* (2019) & watching *Midsommar* on a first date & holding her hands on a second date, on stage at The Glory, & doing the *Midsommar* joint-scream.

---

3   Baudrillard, Jean. *Simulacra and Simulation*

The theatrics of emotion when we perform them together, when we let each other scream.

Hayley Kiyoko's Bed: I have the dreamy, Hayley Kiyoko song *Sleepover* song in my head when the four of us share a bed – sad, soggy-drunk & wobbly with valium, our friend in the hospital. The song is textbook sapphic yearning but here I am hearing this longing in a platonic context: a place of imperfect, platonic comfort in a time of absolute crisis. *Come on let's sleep in my bed / Can I just be in my head with you?*

Moments of crisis call for communal bedtime & sometimes we are all still sad & lonely children standing in the doorways of our mum's bedrooms, asking to come in.

Bobby Parker's Bed: *love will be/ slow & strange again/ you will not care/ it will fit anywhere/ a sweet woozy god of a thing/ you knock empty bottles/ spinning sideways/ into the sun/ as you leap out of bed/ dragging the covers behind you/ to stand/ sequinting at her fat/ naked/ body.*

Tracy Emin's Bed: When I think of the dichotomy of the solitudes & intimacies of beds, I think of Tracy Emin's most famous installations, *My Bed* & *Everyone I Have Slept With*. I relate to *My Bed* deeply, over the years my beds have looked like various incarnations of *My Bed* in my many depressive episodes & when Emin writes, in her autobiography *Strangeland, it was my bed that held me, saved me,* I relate to the cove of bed, the refuge. In *Everyone I Have Slept With,* Emin shows beds as places of intimacies in every sense – familial, platonic, romantic, sexual.

Sophie Robinson's Bed: *if i lie on my back & you lie on your front & we are in the same bed is that sex.*

In the tent, there are no hierarchies of intimacy. On the assumption of the piece as a list of everyone the artist has had sex with, Emin says,

> Some I'd had a shag with in bed or against a wall some I had just slept with, like my grandma. I used to lay in her bed and hold her hand. We used to listen to the radio together and nod off to sleep. You don't do that with someone you don't love and don't care about.

In bed we are grandmotherly with each other or in bed we are post-sex talking about all the bad things we have done or in bed we are hungover watching *Saturday Kitchen* or in bed you call me a worm because I am worming around so much or in bed we wake up at 4am & watch *Eastenders* fights compliations on Youtube or in bed we are in bed together because I can't sleep alone right now or in bed we drink pina colada & have sad-sex for four days or in bed we slap each other round the face & feel weird about it & then laugh about it or in bed I cry about someone else & you pretend not to hear & it is kind of you or in bed I imagined you in this bed so many times before you are here & you are here & it is great or in bed I am taking a picture of you on my phone because I have told myself this will be the last time I will ever see you or in bed we are eating a Mcdonalds breakfast & I wish every day could start so slow & greasy or in bed I feel a bit sick & you are stroking my hair & I first realise I am so in love with you or in bed we are twelve years old watching a sex scene on the little bedroom telly & trying to imagine what sex will be like, if we will ever want it at all or in bed we have drank so many cans how did this happen or in bed we spend all night trying not to have sex or in bed we are eating the prized slab of brie I have brought home from work or in bed you say *do you still think you're not fucked? It's eight in the morning & you've been talking about Corbyn for three hours.*

Emin says, of the reaction to *Everyone I Have Slept With,*

> People were inside the tent, by the time they came out, they were thinking about all the people *they'd* slept with, the people *they'd* been close to. And that's how the tent worked.

Carmen Maria Machado's Bed: *One boy, one girl. My friends. We drank stolen wine coolers in my room, on the vast expanse of my bed.*

Frank O'Hara's Bed: *Put out your hand/ isn't there/an ashtray, suddenly, there? beside the bed? And someone you love enters the room/and says wouldn't you like the eggs a little different today?/And when they arrive they are just plain scrambled eggs and the warm weather is holding.*

The bed of my dreams is the bed in *Bedknobs and Broomsticks,* the flying bed. I think of this when reading Eimar McBride's *The Lesser Bohemians.* In the novel, there is a seventy page scene in which the couple lie in bed, smoking, drinking & Stephan tells Eily the story of his childhood sexual abuse. It is here the characters are first named.

In bed, there are always nights like this, staring at the ceiling, talking till sunrise, where everything changes. These are the things we can say to each other in the dark.

My Bed: At six in the morning, you come back to bed carrying a glass of water for us to share. You are you-shaped in the dark & we are wide eyed, exhausted babies. We go to sleep.

Contributors

Isabel Waidner is a writer and critical theorist. Their novel *We Are Made Of Diamond Stuff* was shortlisted for the Goldsmiths Prize 2019 and the Republic of Consciousness Prize 2020. Their writing has appeared in journals including AQNB, Frieze, The Happy Hypocrite and Tripwire. Waidner is a co-founder of Queers Read This at the Institute of Contemporary Arts, London.

Peter Scalpello is a poet and sexual health therapist from Glasgow, currently living and working in East London. His work has been published internationally, and his debut pamphlets will be published by Broken Sleep Books in March 2021. Tweets @p_scalpello.

Mads Hartley grew up in Burnley and is now based in North London. They are the Copy Editor for an LGBT charity and occasional DJ for queer club nights. They currently spend their time cycling, watching *Desperate Housewives* and grappling with an overly ambitious fiction project. @maddy_hartley

Elizabeth Lovatt is a writer living in London. Her work has featured in Popshot Magazine, 2019's National Flash Fiction Anthology and 404 Ink, among others. She is part of the queer writing collective Futures in the Making and in 2019 she was writer-in-residence at Islington Pride and the rukus! Archive. She is currently studying for an MA in Creative and Critical Writing at Birkbeck and is the Book Buyer at the V&A.

Saurabh Sharma is a writer, currently working for a research and advisory IT consultancy firm. He writes on gender and sexuality, and reviews books. Instagram: @writerly_life; @saurabh_angira.

Cleo Henry is a writer and researcher based in London. She is particularly interested in queerness, radical kinship and the apocalypse. She is currently writing a collection imagining different ways queerness could look like without shame.

Erica Gillingham is a queer poet and writer living in London, England, via Northern California. She is a bookseller at Gay's the Word Bookshop, Books Editor for DIVA Magazine, and has a PhD in lesbian love stories in young adult literature and graphic novels.

Gabrielle Johnson lives in London and works in publishing. She writes psychological and sometimes speculative fiction, most often telling love stories with sad endings. She is passionate about championing queer voices, and is the co-founder and editor of clavmag, a digital lit mag publishing creative writing by queer, trans and non-binary people. Find her on Twitter @gabrielleMCJ.

Sam J Grudgings is a poet perpetually on the edge of collapse. Shortlisted for the Outspoken Poetry Prize, and forever yelling poems at audiences, he is now available in mint choc chip flavour at all good stores.

Adam Zmith is a London Writers Awardee who, for two years, has been working on a novel set after a pandemic. Oh, shit. He is also a co-producer on The Log Books podcast and the literature programme for Fringe! Queer Film and Arts Fest. @AdamZmith on Twitter and @adam.zmith on Instagram.

Helen Savage writes poetry and prose. Her submission 'The Matter' forms part of a larger series she is working on concerning an austerity affected workplace. She lives in London.

Georgie Henley is an actor and writer, born in Yorkshire and currently living in London. This is her first chapbook publication.

Annie Dobson is a graduate of MA Creative and Critical Writing. Her work has appeared in Ambit, The Bi-Ble, RS21 and Spam Press among others. She lives in London.